Congratulations!

You Are Self-Employed

Part Two – Starting an Online Business

By Nancy N. Wilson

Publisher's Notes

Congratulations! You Are Self-Employed
Part Two – Starting an Online Business
By Nancy N. Wilson

Cover by creativelog

© Blurtigo Holdings, LLC
1st Edition – May 2016
Published in United States of America
ISBN-13: 978-1533067432

Disclaimer and Terms of Use:
The Author and Publisher have strived to be as accurate and complete as possible in the creation of this book. While all attempts have been made to verify information provided in this publication, the Author and Publisher assume no responsibility for errors, omissions, or contrary interpretation of the subject matter herein. Perceived slights of specific persons, peoples, or organizations are unintentional.

This material is designed to provide general information about the subject matter covered. The author and publisher are not engaged in rendering legal, financial, medical, or psychological advice. If expert assistance is required in these areas, the services of a professional should be sought.

IMAGES

Thank You – © Peterfactors - Fotolia.com

Start My Own Business - © adrian_ilie825 - Fotolia.com

Shiny Object Syndrome – Adam Short

Home Office – ©Wollwerth Imagery – Big Stock.com

Do Not Disturb Sign – © Ieva – BigStock.com

Self-employed Concept ©venimo – BigStock.com

… for buying my book.
If you enjoy it, please take a minute and post a review
on the platform where you made your purchase

Congratulations!
You Are Self-Employed
Part Two – Starting an Online Business

For a complete list of my published books,
please, visit my website
http://www.nancynwilson.com

Nancy N. Wilson

LIKE My Page on Facebook
https://www.facebook.com/NancyNWilsonAuthor/

Dedication

To everyone who has a deep desire to start
and run a business . . . to be the boss. May you
have great success at building your business
and doing something you love for many years
to come!

Table of Contents

Introduction

Congratulations! You are now the boss!

How does it feel? Maybe a bit overwhelming, but definitely exciting. You can't wait to get started, but you are terrified at the same time. You may be a mixed bag of emotions – or you may be among the few who are perfectly calm, thinking that you have it all under control.

Regardless of how you are feeling, there are some basic things you must consider in order to start the business with a solid foundation.

My book, _**Navigating the Internet Jungle – Proceed with Caution**_ (Part One – Starting an Online Business) covers the potential dangers you may face as you enter the Internet Business World.

This is Part Two and covers only one important component – **being self-employed** – by exploring two basic questions:

1. What does it mean to be self-employed?
2. What is required to get started?

The idea of being your own boss has great appeal, but you can only experience the joy in that experience if you fully understand and prepare for the risks.

Not everyone has the right temperament and personality to stay the course and be successful. You may want to review the "Characteristics Shared by the Successful" found in the first book: *__Navigating the Internet Jungle__*.

Being self-employed carries a unique set of challenges. The primary purpose of this book is to make you aware of the basics steps you should take in order to establish a solid business base.

It will also give you direction and a few tools to help you complete the steps

The primary focus of this book is individuals who want to start an Online business; but, the information could be applied to any type of business.

My Story

My first entrepreneurial venture began in 1978 when I bought a wallpaper shop and started my own interior design consulting firm.

Fortunately, I had a good friend and accountant who helped me with the financial side of the business and I was married to an attorney who helped with the legal side.

Even with their advice I took a few missteps and paid dearly for them, but I was wise enough to learn from my mistakes, which paid dividends over the years. I have applied those lessons with each new business that I established.

I have been self-employed most of my professional life, with only a few side journeys as an employee for other companies.

Two Important Lessons:

1. I am a much better solo act than I am when I am directed and micromanaged by someone else.

2. Taking care of business when I am self-employed is vital to my success and financial stability.

The second lesson is why I put together this small book to help others who are also better as an entrepreneur (self-employed) than they are as an employee.

My hope is that the information, which is based on my years of experience, will be helpful to you.

All the best,

Nancy

Chapter 1
What It Means to Be Self-Employed

You Are the Business

If you are reading this book it is probable that you are ready already to your own business, or are seriously considering it. Either way, it is critical to have a clear understanding of **what it means to be self-employed.**

The bottom line is that in the beginning you will be working more hours for less money than you were making (or could make) working for someone else.

Plus, it will be difficult to separate yourself from the business because **you are the business.** You will be on-call 24/7.

The appeal of being self-employed and working from home sounds glorious and exciting, but many who express that desire have little understanding of what is actually involved.

I have heard people say, "I want to own my own business so I can work when I want and play when I want."

You CAN do that if you choose . . . BUT, as a self-employed person you will quickly learn that if you don't work, you don't get paid.

There is definitely an upside when you choose to start your own business – and become **the boss**. But, there is also a downside.

Let's take a look at both sides.

The Upside (Pros)

- You are the boss. (No one is watching over your shoulder or telling you what to do and when to do it.)
- Your income is not capped by a salary level, but by what you produce. (This is a pro <u>and</u> a con.)
- You set your own hours. (You can choose to work, or not.)
- There is no glass ceiling. (For women entrepreneurs.)
- There are no limits on what you can accomplish.
- You have creative freedom.
- If something isn't working, you can change it without asking anyone.
- You reap the rewards. (Hopefully, there are rewards to reap.)
- You are always learning – and developing new skills as you face the challenges that come with being self-employed.
- Vacation time is flexible. (If you are disciplined and focused, you may choose to work a three- or four-day week and take the other days off.)
- You can choose your working partners, colleagues, etc.
- If you don't want to do business with someone, you don't have to.
- You work in a more relaxed working environment.
- Eat whatever you want, whenever you want.
- Have an indoor or outdoor office – window/no window – it is your choice.

- Traveling to and from work is no longer a necessity or expense.
- Maintaining a large up-to-date wardrobe is no longer needed. Any attire is acceptable and no makeup or shave is required.
- No expense for daycare. (This one depends on your situation)

The Downside (Cons)

- You are the boss – the buck stops with you. (There is no one to blame for mistakes.)
- You take all the risks (personal, mental, emotional, and financial).

- The security of the paycheck is gone. (When you are self-employed your income stream can be unpredictable, you must learn to live with that.)
- Your income is not capped by salary level, but by what you produce. (Could be a pro or con)
- You will have to convince your family and friends that you really do have a job.
- In the beginning, when you have no staff, you wear all the hats (can be overwhelming).
- You pay all of your FICA tax (your employer used to pay half).
- Estimated quarterly taxes must be paid.
- You have to buy health insurance, which is typically either very expensive or the coverage is lousy. (If you

are lucky, you spouse will still have company coverage.)

- You must be organized and keep very good records. (For disorganized people this is a big con.)
- You will need an accountant you trust (to do your tax return) and a good attorney – maybe not on retainer, but at least someone you can call when you have questions. (This is only a con because of the cost.)
- The working environment can be challenging with continuous distractions and disruptions. Depending on your home situation (family, or not) and your level of self-discipline, you may accomplish a great deal more or a significant amount less in a work day than you typically accomplished in a brick and mortar office.

As mentioned in the introduction, I have had my own business more years than not over my professional life.

Being self-employed and working from home is the best choice for me because I do not work well under the direction of someone else over the long term.

I need creative freedom and the ability to make my own decisions – good and bad; and I am willing and able to take the consequences.

I have also learned how to manage and live with an erratic income, which is difficult for some personality types.

Even though I had my own brick and mortar business in the past, the ideal model for me now is Online.

I write, self-publish, and market my books, research and write my blogs, manage my Websites, and serve my coaching clients.

I usually work eight to ten hours a day, five or six days a week, and enjoy the option of working anywhere (in my office, in my living room, on the patio, at the library, or at Starbucks). All I need is an Internet connection.

I also have the flexibility of working through the weekend and taking a day off in the middle of the week to run errands and do my shopping. Having an adjustable schedule is the best!

The online model works for many types of businesses – coaching, marketing, training, virtual assistant, retail sales, consulting, editing, speaking, writing, publishing . . . and the list goes on.

Developing a lucrative online business is not easy. It takes time to grow the business and to begin generating a decent income.

Success does not come overnight; but with patience, self-discipline, and focus, you can do it and be successful.

Even if you have to make several attempts to find the right formula for you, it is worth the effort when the business model fits your personality.

If working from home – being your own boss – is your dream and you have the right personality/temperament for it, you can make it your reality.

Chapter 2
The Legal Side of Things

Structuring Your Business

One of the most important decisions you will make is what type of legal structure to select. Even if you have decided to run a very small business on Ebay or through your own Website, you should still establish yourself as a business entity.

State and Federal laws require that you claim all business income of over $400 annually. The government wants their share.

Setting up a legal structure for your company may seem like an unnecessary expense in the beginning, but you should seriously consider doing it anyway.

The legal structure you choose will impact how much you pay in taxes, your personal liability, and much more. Plus every account you establish in connection with your business that involves the exchange of money will require designation of your legal structure.

Be sure to consult with an attorney who has expertise in business structures as they apply to Online businesses and e-commerce.

Using an attorney friend who does not have the proper knowledge or trying to do it yourself to save money would not be a good decision. Making the wrong choice could end up being costly; and changing the structure later may prove to be difficult.

The Four Most Common Business Entities

Sole Proprietor

This is the most common type of legal structure for a business that is owned and operated by one person. It is the easiest and lowest cost to set-up because of the limited legal formalities involved; but, also has the least amount of legal protection.

Limited Liability Company (LLC)

The LLC combines benefits of a corporation and a partnership – but can be used even if you are a one-person company.

It establishes a legal separation between your business and personal assets, which means that your personal assets are protected if you get sued or have business debts. The set-up costs are reasonable.

Partnerships

There are general partnerships and limited partnerships. A partnership is used when one or more people will share the profits and losses of the business.

Partnerships can be complicated and must suit your needs. Everyone involved must be very clear and in agreement with the terms of the partnership – make no assumptions or problems can arise very quickly. One of the biggest risks in all partnerships is the possibility of disagreement or unrest among partners.

Corporations

There are two types of corporations, the S-corporation and the C-corporation. This structure is used when there are shareholders or other investors – and for larger companies with employees.

Although it is best to seek *advice and assistance of a legal professional,* you may want more information before you choose to finalize he structure of your business.

I have provided a few additional resources below for information purposes only – not as formal recommendations.

Online Sources of Legal Information

LegalZoom – An online resource that allows you to complete legal paperwork for both DBAs (Doing Business As) and LLCs (Limited Liability Company) online. The site also provides an education center with articles and videos that can help you with the process

Internal Revenue Service – The IRS Website explains each of the business entities.

SCORE.org - This is a free Online resource for business owners that provide almost unlimited information on all things business - including great information on legal business entities.

Banking

Business Checking (or Savings) Account

Once you have selected the structure and completed all the necessary paper work, you should also open up a separate business checking and/or savings account.

It is a good idea to have all monies generated by the business paid as direct deposits into this account. This creates a clear division between personal and business accounts and will ensure that you are paying quarterly estimated tax payments based on your income (as required by law).

Tax Laws

Business Taxes

Investigate this carefully. You do not want to be on the wrong side of the law when it comes to taxes. There may be a local business tax and reports that you will need to file when you run a business out of your home.

I have listed the most common ones below.

Sales Tax

If you are selling merchandise, even electronic merchandise, you may be responsible for collecting and reporting sales tax. You should be clear about this before you make your first sale.

When sales tax is required, the seller should collect it from the buyer of the merchandise at the time of the sale; and then, the seller must report and pay the tax to the state and/or local tax entities.

You also need a state retail sales license, which requires a return to be filed monthly.

For example: In Arizona it is called a "Transaction Privilege, Use, and Severance Tax Return.

Check your state requirements and follow the guidelines exactly.

PLEASE NOTE: The state will expect payment on all taxable sales whether you collect the tax or not. If it is not paid in a timely manner, you will have to pay not only the amount you should have collected from customers, but fines and penalties, as well.

Income and Social Security Taxes

If being self-employed is a new experience for you, be aware that you – and you alone – are responsible for reporting your income and paying your taxes.

You absolutely MUST educate yourself about what this means and do everything necessary to cover the bases.

Talk to a good accountant and set up a plan for paying *estimated income tax* or you could be in for a big, unpleasant surprise at tax time.

No one told me about estimated income tax when I opened my first business in California – many years ago. I was incredibly successful and generated a wonderful income stream that I happily spent.

At tax time, I was hit with a $12,000 tax bill. It was a huge grey financial cloud that hovered over me for the next two years as I paid off the bill, while also paying estimated income tax for the current years. Do not let this happen to you!

If you are making a lot of money – estimate your income on the generous side. Your accountant should be able to give you an educated estimate of what you should pay.

Since my $12,000 snafu, I have always placed 30% of my income in a separate savings account that is untouchable. My estimated taxes are always paid from that account. This has prevented a repeat problem for me in this area.

FYI - The following information was taken directly from the Social Security Administration Website:

http://www.socialsecurity.gov/pubs/EN-05-10022.pdf

> *Most people who pay into Social Security work for an employer. Their employer deducts Social Security taxes from their paycheck, matches that contribution and sends taxes to the Internal Revenue Service (IRS) and reports wages to Social Security. But self-employed people must report their earnings and pay their taxes directly to the IRS.*
>
> *If you are self-employed, if you operate a trade, business or profession, either by yourself or as a partner, you report your earnings for Social Security when you file your federal income tax return. **If your net earnings are $400 or more in a year, you must report your earnings on Schedule SE in addition to the other tax forms you must file.***
>
> *The Social Security tax rate for 2013 is 15.3 percent on self-employment income up to $113,700. If your net earnings exceed $113,700, you continue to pay only the Medicare portion of the Social Security tax, which is 2.9 percent, on the rest of your earnings. However, effective with this tax year, the Medicare tax rate increases 0.9 percent from its current rate of 2.9 percent to 3.8 percent on net earnings*

In other words, you are responsible for filing quarterly reports for estimated earnings and making payments to the IRS based on those estimates.

The government does not care whether you know about the law, or not. Ignorance is not bliss, in this case – it is dangerous.

Other Legal Issues

Zoning Laws

If you are a one-man (or woman) shop – working alone on your personal computer, you probably do not need to worry about this issue.

It is unlikely that you will be affected by zoning laws, restrictions of an owner's association, or a tenant agreement; but, it may be good to check anyway.

However, if you plan to store inventory, ship merchandise; or have employees, you MUST check the local zoning laws for restrictions that may be part of your homeowner's association agreement or tenant's agreement or lease.

Be sure to take this step and protect yourself. Neighbors can be finicky and violation of such restrictions could be a big problem if you were reported.

Business Licenses and Permits

You may or may not need these, but you should check. Requirements will vary by city and state and the type of business you will be running.

A good place to start is with the U.S. Small Business Administration: http://www.sba.gov/licenses-and-permits.

Copyrights

You must protect your intellectual property with a copyright. Copyright law protects original works of authorship, including books, articles, plays, music, poetry, songs, photography, computer software and architecture. Copyrights cover published and unpublished works.

It does not protect facts, ideas, systems, or methods of operation.

It is different from a patent that protects inventions or discoveries; and from trademarks that protect words, phrases, symbols or designs used by people or companies to brand their goods and services.

Your work is protected from the moment it is created in tangible form and does not have to be registered to be legal; but, in case of a lawsuit for infringement of work, registration would be important.

You need to understand copyright law for two reasons:

1. If you will be producing anything that fits into one of the categories mentioned above requiring a copyright – be sure to get the necessary information and put the copyright in place.

2. If you use photos, art work, materials, etc. that are copyrighted by others on your Website or blog, etc. be sure to purchase the correct license for your intended use; and, stay in compliance by giving proper attribution.

I have never been sued on this issue, but I did have a book tied up for a period of time and ran into problem with Amazon because of it – so, be careful

Don't break the law on this one. It can cost you. Just because you found the image on the Internet, does not mean that it is free or public domain material.

For more information on copyright law, check with the U. S. Copyright Office or LegalZoom.

Disclaimer: *The information in this chapter is for educational purposes only – to alert you to things you should investigate.*

I urge you to seek advice from qualified, licensed experts in order to fully protect yourself. I suggest that you find and confer with an attorney and a good tax accountant.

Chapter 3
It Is Important to Be Organized

Keep Good Records

Do not be the person who shows up at the accountant's office with a box full of notes and receipts. Even if you have never done it before, you absolutely MUST KEEP GOOD RECORDS for your business.

Track everything!

- Income from every source
- Get receipts for every expenditure. (Mark them clearly - where spent, purpose and circle the amount.)

Develop a system that allows you to record and track your finances in a systematic and orderly fashion – either on a daily, weekly, monthly basis – BUT, the longer the period, the most difficult the task.

Talk to your accountant. Find out exactly what s/he will need.

Do not put yourself in a position of meeting with your accountant at tax time and discovering that you are missing critical information and have no idea how to find it.

(BTW – unless you are very up-to-date on tax law, I do not recommend that you do your own income tax reports.)

You also never want to find yourself sitting in the office of an IRS representative for an audit without being well-armed with detailed records. Ignorance of the law has never been and will never be accepted as an excuse for not having the proper documentation for your taxes. The government does not care!

The amount you could pay in penalties and fines could be more than the tax itself. Keep good records!

Find the Right Tools or Get Help

When you are newly self-employed (especially on the Internet), it is easy to get caught up in the excitement of it all. But, you must protect yourself legally and financially. Both are critical for your long-term success.

Do the research and hire people to help you or buy quality tools and learn how to use them.

Get outside help in areas that you cannot or should not try to do yourself – two big ones: legal questions and tax accounting.

Many people handle the day-to-day record keeping themselves, which is usually OK until the business gets too large. However, if you have no bookkeeping or accounting knowledge – or are incredibly bad at it, it would be wise (if at all possible) to hire someone to keep financial records for you.

Another alternative is to hire someone to help you set up a system; and you take it from there.

Set Up Your Systems Early

Whether you choose to do it yourself or to hire someone, the earlier you set up your system, the better – preferably from the very beginning. DO NOT wait until tax time to try to pull it all together. If possible, choose someone who lives close and who is compatible with your personality.

With an electronic accounting system such as Quickbooks or Quicken or another similar online accounting program, you may be able to keep your own records There are also free programs such as Microsoft Money, which is often included when you purchase a new computer.

My personal preference is Quicken. But, be forewarned, there is a learning curve involved and if you have no bookkeeping or accounting experience, learning how to use the program could be time consuming and frustrating.

Ask your friends about their experiences with accounting programs, and read reviews. Find one that seems to fit your needs the best. Some are loaded with features that you won't need in the beginning and may never need; others may not have enough features – so do your homework. Too much of a good thing (excessive unused features) slows down your computer and drains resources. Choose carefully.

Organize Your Files

In addition to keeping good financial records, you will also need to have an effective system for storing information on your computer. Be as organized and consistent as possible in labeling files.

You should also keep a master list of log or some kind so that files are easy to find. Don't try to keep it all in your head. You may think you will remember, but you won't.

Files that you may need: *(Most of these can be e-files on your computer; but, there are a few that you may want to have back-up hardcopies, such as contracts and legal documents.)*

- **Inventory and tracking of purchases** – software, training, books, etc. (including all receipts).
- **Cost of doing business** - equipment, supplies, contract employees, telephone, Internet, etc. (Keep all your receipts).
- **Income from all sources** (including any documentation that you receive)
- **E-mails and Instant Messaging** – be sure to save all business related conversations. Set up the necessary files on your e-mail server and your instant messaging program.
- **Business contacts** – names, addresses, phone numbers and email addresses, plus the name of their companies, notes of telephone conversations, emails to them and from them, etc. Outlook 2010 with Business

Contact Manager is available with Office Professional Plus 2010 and Office Standard 2010.

- **Media contacts** – names, addresses, phone numbers and email addresses, plus the names of the radio or TV stations, newspapers or magazines they work for, telephone conversation notes, emails to and from them, etc.
- **Information and training sources** (anything you buy and may want to return)
- **Proposals sent**
- **Proposals received**
- **Contracts and Legal Documents of all Kinds**
- **Articles written** – where they were submitted and results of the submission, including publication dates and sites.
- **E-books** – have separate folders for:

  → Book Ideas

  → Books in Progress

  → Published Books (with copyright information, publication date, ISBN and ASIN numbers, publisher, editors, illustrators, etc.).

  → Have a file for each book with the covers and final copies of every format you used and submitted to publishers: Original Word format, MOBI, E-Pub, PDF, etc.

→ If you feel compelled to keep old versions, place them in a file that is clearly identified as "OLD VERSIONS." Frankly, it is better to delete them to avoid confusion and limit the clutter on your computer.

The list above is by no means comprehensive and should be used as an example.

The files you will need to set up and maintain will vary depending on the work you do or the type of business you have.

Figure out what you need and create your systems immediately. Don't worry about having everything perfect. You can always adjust and expand as you go.

30

Chapter 4
Protect Yourself and Your Business

Unfortunately, working at home on the Internet carries its own set of dangers that also requires taking precautions, paying attention, and avoiding situations that could put you in harm's way. You must protect yourself and protect your business.

As discussed in Part One, there are many Internet crooks whose one and only goal is to convince you to buy products you don't need, will probably never use, and are not worth the money. They guarantee that their product will solve your problem, save you time, and help you make "six figures in six weeks."

The shortcuts they offer are never really shortcuts. Their methods of selling are incredibly seductive as you continuously struggle with the daily challenges of trying to get where you want to be.

Avoid the Shiny Object Syndrome

The Shiny Object Syndrome is possibly the most common distraction for people who are new to doing business on the Internet.

One of the most important lessons to be learned is how to identify a real business opportunity and how to recognize offers that are nothing more than distractions that can pull you off course and result in the loss of time and money.

As you get more and more involved in your business, regardless of your area of focus – Social Media Marketing, E-commerce, Writing, Publishing, Virtual Assistant, Website Design, Affiliate Marketing, etc. – you will be bombarded with offers that promise to "help you be successful." You must always ask the question,

"Is this purchase I am about to make a strategic business decision or a costly distraction?"

The solution to this problem, or maybe I should say the preventative action to help you avoid developing the "shiny object syndrome" is two-fold:

1. **Choose one strategy and stay with it long enough to see results** (a minimum of six months – preferably a year.) When you are first starting out, learn as much as you can about your area of interest – starting with the free information available on the Internet.

    After you have thoroughly digested the FREE information - then, and only then should you consider purchasing products or training of any kind.

2. **Do not allow yourself to be distracted**. DO NOT "buy-in" to every offer that comes along just because it sounds good and you HOPE that it will solve all your problems and kick-start the money train.

    The only method that works for me to control this distraction is to automatically "unsubscribe" and delete every "sales" message that I receive. DO NOT READ THEM.

Keep your long-term goal(s) in mind at all times. Goals should always be considered in the purchase of books, training programs, software, or other materials. *If the material does not tie-in directly with the accomplishment of your goals and the strategy that you are currently using . . . do not make the purchase.* It will only be a distraction and take you off course.

REMEMBER – the offer (or one very similar) will always be available if you decide you want to explore it in the future.

Anyone who knows anything about sports (which includes most of us, at least as spectators) has heard the statement, "The best offense is a good defense!"

Your offense consists of having a clear plan for success and being well-informed and well-armed to deal with anyone who would willingly steal from you by selling you worthless programs and information.

For more in-depth coverage on the information in this chapter, read *Navigating the Internet Jungle* – **Proceed with Caution.**

Chapter 5
Putting It All Together

You can pat yourself on the back – even have a small celebration because if you took care of everything in the first three chapters, you have the foundation in place and are almost ready to move forward with your online business.

There are still a few more very important things you must do.

Write Your Business Plan

No smart business person would plunge ahead with a new venture unless s/he had a clear plan in place that included goals (long-term and short-term) and action steps that can move him or her forward, one step at a time, toward the goals.

In other words, you need to develop a **business plan**.

Do not let those two words frighten you – it doesn't have to be an elaborate fully-fleshed out, professional business plan. I realize that your ultimate long-term goals may not be completely clear in the beginning, but you must be clear about what you generally want to accomplish in the long term.

With that big picture in mind you should be able to develop more specific goals (a plan – including actions steps) for the next three months that will begin moving you in the right direction.

As you near the end of the three months, you should develop a plan for the next three (or possibly six) months.

Your end game should become clearer as time goes by. Be sure to evaluate, at least monthly. Make adjustments to your plan based on what you have learned through both your successes and your failures (mistakes).

If your goals are defined and refined regularly; and you keep them uppermost in your mind when making decisions, they can bring you back to reality when you may be tempted to take a path that is not in your best interests.

They can also save you a lot of money by preventing you from purchasing materials, training, software, etc. that are not directly in line with what you are trying to accomplish.

Have Your Own Designated Work Space

It is very important to have your own work space – preferably a separate room that is specifically designated as your office and has a door than can be closed when you are working.

If a separate room is not possible, the next best choice is a corner of a room that is used for other things but that has a door that can be closed during your scheduled working hours.

Be creative! A large closet can be transformed into a very efficient workspace. One with doors that can be closed to keep your work untouched when you are not around is perfect.

Create a Schedule and Follow It

Get Up and Go to Work

When you are self-employed you must keep regular working hours. You get up and go to work every day whether you want to or not – five days a week minimum as a rule.

The key to success is discipline. Your livelihood depends on it. If you do not work, you will not get paid! (The best part is that you do not have to get up and shower, shave or put on make-up, and travel miles to get to work.)

It is important to set scheduled working hours. Plan exactly how you will use the time and stick to the schedule. You need a starting time, breaks, lunch, and a quitting time - follow it as closely as possible every day.

Your new online business is now your JOB! Stay at that desk until the day is done. Take breaks every hour or two (but short ones) and stop for lunch. Set a time limit for both and stay within the limit. If you don't – 10 minute breaks can turn into an hour and a 30-minute lunch can turn into the whole afternoon.

Avoid distractions of all kinds – including TV in the background.

Setting a schedule and sticking to it can be a big challenge for the newly self-employed who are working at home. No one is looking over your shoulder, so if you live alone, you have to deal with the temptation to "watch just one program on TV" or have that second (or third) cup of coffee before you sit down to work.

If you have a family, you have to deal with the possibility of frequent interruptions, noise, and unexpected distractions.

Enlist your family's support by asking them to agree to respect your schedule and understand that during working hours you are unavailable.

Depending on your family's situation, your working hours may have to be early morning and after the children's bedtime in the evening. Figure out a plan that makes sense and then, make it happen.

The more disciplined and consistent you are, the more your family will accept that you *are working – just as you always have.* They will eventually realize the only difference is that you are doing it at home.

Just because you are not bound by someone else's "clock" does not mean that you are free to do whatever you feel like doing throughout the day. In fact, no one making demands on your time is the very reason that having a daily plan to follow becomes doubly important.

If you do not have a plan and flit from one thing to another, randomly doing whatever comes to mind, you are setting yourself up for problems. *Disorganization results in low productivity and potential failure in the long-run.*

A plan for how you will use your working hours can be as simple as dividing your day into blocks of time and assigning a category of work to each chunk of time. I also recommend that at the end of each day you fill in the tasks that must be accomplished in each category for the next day (always prioritizing, of course).

If you have no idea how to do this, there are many scheduling programs available on the Internet – some of them are free. Personally, I use the Google Calendar that includes daily reminders of what I should be doing at certain times of the day. Depending on your level of self-discipline and your experience in working alone and unsupervised, that may be too broad and open for you. You may want something more structured.

Many of the work scheduling programs come with a built-in 'to-do' list option, which can be very helpful. I know from experience how easy it is to get side-tracked and succumb to the temptations of "doing other things" when you are working at home.

A **solid work ethic**, **self-discipline** and the **ability to stay focused** (on-point) are three key characteristics that you will find in all successful self-employed people. If those characteristics are already part of your make-up, you are WAY ahead of the game. If not, the faster you develop them, the faster you will realize the success you are seeking.

Let Everyone Know – This Is Your Real Job

Your friends and family may not understand what you are doing and may even give you a hard time about finding "a real job." When you are sitting in front of your computer all day and trekking through the Internet Jungle – struggling to find your way, it may appear to others that you are not doing much – and wasting your time.

These people (family and friends) are not the enemy.... at least they don't mean to be the enemy; nor do they mean any real harm; but, since they have never done what you are doing and do not understand the process, they have a hard time seeing it as a real job. They may assume that you are unemployed and passing time by amusing yourself on your computer.

One of the problems that can develop from their erroneous assumptions is that since you are not busy, you should be available and willing to run errands for them, talk to them on the telephone, or have a pot of coffee ready whenever they decide to drop in unannounced at all times of the day.

These problematic infringements on your time are easier to combat when you are clear about your goals; and you have a work schedule in place that you follow religiously.

There should be no question in their minds (or yours) about what you are doing. You may even have to lay down specific rules about when you are available and when you are not.

A *"do not disturb"* sign on the door can be very effective. You should also make it clear that when the sign is on the doorknob, the only acceptable form of communication is texting, to which you will not reply unless it is an emergency.

Be Disciplined and Consistent

Every worthwhile endeavor requires disciplined consistency of action. I am sure that you have experienced the reality of this at different points in your life; but, it is possible that you have not yet connected the principles of self-discipline and consistency with being self-employed and running an online business. But, I guarantee that both are just as important in this arena as they have been in all other aspects of your life.

Watch for Tipping Points

Think back to when you learned to ride a bike. Remember that feeling when all of a sudden something "clicked" in your head and suddenly you were flying down the street all by yourself with no one holding the back of the bike?

Or – what about when you learned to swim and suddenly everything worked? For the first time you felt the exhilaration of being completely free and powerful in the water.

Such moments of "knowing" are called tipping points. It is when all the hard work and effort come together and tip the scales in your favor. You begin to reap the rewards of your effort. This is when the stress eases, the work begins to flow, and the rewards multiply.

Accomplishing goals of any kind – physical, mental, emotional, financial, etc. – requires self-discipline together with consistent and focused effort. You must be willing to invest the necessary time and effort for as long as it takes, without letting up, until you succeed.

Developing this kind of disciplined consistency is usually most difficult in the beginning. You will never reach the tipping point with your online business if you are not willing and able to put forth consistent and focused effort over an extended period of time.

Success Takes Time

Regardless of what the "Internet Gurus" tell you, online *success takes time – it does not happen overnight, or even over a few weeks. It usually takes years.*

How long did it take you to learn to ride a bike? (Longer than you wanted it to, I am sure.) How many times did you fall in the process? If you were a typical kid, it was probably more than once. What if you had given up after the first fall, or the second, or even the third and decided it wasn't worth it? The answer is simple; you would never have learned to ride a bike and you would have missed out on one of the great joys of childhood.

Learn from Mistakes and Setbacks

As a newbie in the Online business world, you will undoubtedly make mistakes and have setbacks. You will experience failures and may frequently feel as if you are in over your head. You may even reach the point where you believe that it is not worth it and you want to give up. Take heart, my fellow Internet jungle explorer; you will be in good company. Practically everyone who ventures into the Internet Jungle experiences the same thing. If you can discipline yourself to remain consistent in your effort and never let your focus falter as you continue to work, you will reach your goals.

Review and Celebrate Successes

At the end of each day, review your successes, no matter how small; make notes on lessons learned; prioritize your list of things to do tomorrow; and put your fears and concerns out of your mind for the evening. Turn your full attention to your family, your friends, your hobbies, etc. Relax and refresh your mind, body, and spirit so that you are ready to begin again in the morning.

Keep Work and Home Responsibilities Separate

This can be difficult when your office and home are one in the same. There will be some overlap – it can't be avoided. However, you must do everything possible to keep them separate. As mentioned earlier, you must have a work schedule (office hours) and clearly defined family time, with boundaries set for each.

Word of warning: You may be the one who has trouble honoring family time because as the day draws to a close you may find yourself involved in something that you feel compelled to finish before you quit for the evening.

Don't let yourself get caught in that kind of thinking – the project will still be there in the morning. Family time should be just as important as work hours – both should be held sacred.

Learn to Say NO

You may also need to put a lid on your guilt complex (if you have one). You are NOT a terrible person if you don't take three hours out of your work day to take Grammy to her hair appointment. You may be expected to do it because "everybody else is working." Be very clear with others (and yourself) – you are also working! Other arrangements can be made – so make them.

You may need to learn how to say, "No" and to be able to say it effectively. Do not make promises you cannot (or should not) keep when they infringe on your working hours.

Learning to say no in a kind, but firm way takes some practice, but you can learn to do it if you are committed to the success of your new business.

Keep On Keeping On

When you are self-employed, you have to wear all the hats, which is exhausting.

There are simply not enough hours in the day to do everything that must be done. Plus, you must constantly face the reality that there are facets of your business that are not in your wheelhouse! Those tasks can eat up hours of time and basically drive you crazy.

Obviously, the best solution is to hire others to take care of the tasks that challenge you because you do not have the skill set or experience – or – you really don't like to do them (even if you can).

Unfortunately, when you first strike out on your own, cash flow can be so tight that hiring others is not an option and you are forced to do it all.

My recommendations are (if you are forced to do it all):

- **Make a list** of everything that must be done.
- **Categorize the tasks** – 5 or 6 categories are best. (For example: Research and Writing; E-mails/telephone calls/forums/social media; Blog Posts; Marketing/Promotions; Administration)
- **Define necessary time allotments** – Decide what percentage of your day should be allotted for each category, allowing sufficient time for the category that is the core of your business. (For example: As a writer, most of my time must be spent writing.)
- **Prioritize** the tasks within each category.
- **Set up a daily schedule** – allotting the appropriate amount of time for each category.
- **Follow the schedule!**
- **Stop at the end of the allotted time period** and move onto tasks in the next category – always starting with the top priority task.

The keys to success are: organization, discipline, and to keep on keeping on!

Chapter 6
On the Mark! Get Set! Go!

If you have covered all the previous points and implemented the suggestions, you are in good shape.

Below is a check list of what is required to be successful and sustain long-term growth:

- ✓ **Business Plan**: You know exactly where you are today and you know where you want to go (at least the broad strokes). You have a doable business plan that will get you to your first check point - in 3 months, 6 months, one year, three years . . . or as far out as you can see clearly.

- ✓ **Knowledge and Awareness:** Knowledge is power in this business, as it is in any business. Stay current with what is happening in your niche and on the Internet in general. Watch for dangerous pitfalls, internet scoundrels who are willing to take your money and give you little in return, and be aware of your personal demons. Any one of the three can be your downfall, but if you stay alert and develop the tools to handle them, you will be OK.

- ✓ **Training and Tools:** Recognize your weak spots and get help when you need it. Be on the lookout for legitimate products and materials that are directly related to your goals. Learn to recognize the difference between real help and costly distractions. Seek out the first and reject the latter.

✓ **Work from Your Strengths:** Everyone has strengths. Be honest with yourself about yours – and use them. Find others to do the things that you cannot do, or would rather not do (if possible).

See the list below for positive behaviors that can be the foundation of your success.

- **Be Disciplined** – You are now responsible for doing everything – the things you like to do, the things you don't like to do, and everything in-between. Your online business is your job. You must get up, go to work and stay at work all day every day – even when you don't want to and even when you don't feel like it. If you don't do what needs to be done – it won't be done. You cannot be lazy, sloppy, disorganized or indulge in procrastination.

- **Be Consistent:** Success comes from consistent action. You learn by doing – finding out what works and what doesn't work and establishing routines that take you one-step-at-a-time toward your goals.

- **Be Focused:** In order to get where you want to go, you must have a clear picture of your destination. In the words of Stephen Covey, "Begin with the end in mind" and never lose sight of where you want to be.

- **Be Ambitious:** Success as a self-employed person requires full, unrelenting commitment to securing a better life for yourself and for your family. Without that commitment you may not make it. At the same time, do not let ambition blind you and prevent you from making wise decisions and keeping balance in your life.

- **Be Ethical:** This builds a foundation of trust on which all your relationships will be built. This will sound cynical, but ethics seems to be a rare personal characteristic in today's business world. It takes a person with fortitude to practice it when it seems that many around you are not. Be one of the good guys. Promise the best and deliver what you promise – don't take short cuts in anything that you do.

- **Be Determined:** You will face challenges at every turn. You must have the determination to overcome them regardless of how long it takes. One of the biggest challenges is to stay the course when you feel like you are getting nowhere fast!

- **Do Whatever It Takes:** A Herculean work ethic is critical! You must be willing to work as long and as hard as necessary to accomplish your goals. It will help you to keep on keeping on even when you feel overwhelmed, frustrated, or discouraged.

- **in the Time:** To be financially successful over the long haul, working part time will probably not cut it. This is not to say that you should quit your day job immediately, but at some point, you will have to do so. Building a successful business takes time and effort – including forgoing many personal hobbies and pleasures. You must be willing to pay your dues. There is no such a thing as overnight success. There are always years of preparation and hard work that make the success possible.

- **Be Patient:** The resulting speed at which we currently live our lives is primarily due to technology – especially the Internet. Everything is at our fingertips and the ability to be patient is rare. BUT, for the self-employed person who is building a business – patience is critical. Success still takes time. If this is one of your weak points – as it is one of mine – you MUST develop it, no matter how much it hurts. Accomplishing your goals will take as long as it takes . . . and being impatient will simply make it more difficult than it needs to be.

- **Don't Depend on Luck:** There may be some degree of luck in making a business successful; but, I am with some of the old timers on this one – you make your own luck. A strong blend of ambition, determination, a strong work ethic, time, hard work and patience will bring you all the luck you need. I call it getting exactly what you deserve.

Conclusion

Not everyone can do what you are planning to do. Many dream about it, many venture into it, many fail; **but some succeed.**

You can be among the successful group if you have what it takes – beginning with the guts and willingness to jump into the unknown – especially the vast unknown of the Internet.

Those who are *unwilling to accept the status quo* are the ones who change it and make a better future for themselves, their families, and sometimes for the rest of the world. Not being satisfied with "the way things are" is an admirable quality and one that you should be proud to claim. You have this quality or you would never have decided to begin this adventure in the first place.

Develop your plan to make changes in your life; implement your plan; and make adjustments, as necessary. Move forward each day by taking actions that will move you toward your destination.

Telling people, "I want to work at home....or I want my own online business" is NOT a plan. That is nothing more than wishful thinking. Having a big dream is wonderful, but dreaming and wishing does not make it happen.

You must *have a plan* and **work your plan** diligently (revising the plan when necessary) until your big dream becomes a reality.

You must prepare yourself for a long, hard journey, facing every challenge and finding the best solution to every problem.

Facing your own fears can sometime be the biggest challenge of all – your fear of failure (or success). You may also have to deal with frustration that comes with facing obstacle after obstacle, discouragement when things seem to be going wrong, anxiety when you don't know what to do next, and anger when everything takes longer than you think it should.

There are many challenges that come with running your own business, especially on the Internet; and at first glance, some of them may seem insurmountable – but they aren't if you have the strength to "keep on, keeping on."

You will soon learn that the Internet Jungle is ripe with opportunity for those who have the ambition, drive, and determination to venture in and conquer it.

Before we way goodbye, I want to share with you a list from an article in Forbes Magazine titled, *13 Signs You Are Meant To Be Self-Employed*, written by Molly Crane. Click on the link for the full article.

1. You want flexibility in your schedule
2. You want more control over your ideas, your projects, and the work that you do
3. You don't play well with others
4. You have passion for what you do
5. You are a good listener
6. You are comfortable being "the decider"

7. You have a support system
8. You are a disciplined self-starter.
9. You are able and willing to attend events alone
10. You are able to compartmentalize work and private life
11. You have an ability to let things go
12. You can go with the flow
13. You are resourceful

Should You Be Self-employed?

Now that you have digested all the basics requirements of being self-employed, you must answer the question – truthfully.

If you have decided that you should not take this leap, that's OK – at least you found out before you were in too deep.

If the answer is YES, you should be self-employed, get going right now!

The next step is to get your business up and running . . .

So . . . where to begin?

I know how overwhelming it can be when you are first starting out. There is an endless amount of much information and people may be coming at you from all directions, wanting to give you advice and imploring you to buy their product or service. It is difficult to know which way to turn.

As you try to sift through the offerings hoping to find something that will really help you and not break the bank, it can be confusing and discouraging.

A wise first step would be to make good use of all the free information available online.

Also, check out the next two books in this series:

- The Work-at-Home Planning Guide
- Up and Running

If you want personal attention, I am available for one-on-one coaching to help you get through the rough spots. You can reach me at _wilsonemarketing@gmail.com._

Enjoy your new adventure. I am looking forward to seeing your name "up in lights" as we both continue on this exciting journey.

Nancy N. Wilson

About the Author

Nancy N. Wilson

All things beautiful are my passion. I enjoy anything that a masterful hand creates - writing, photography, visual arts, cooking, the human body, the human spirit, technology, our beautiful world and so much more.

As a young child, I was very curious and always wanted to know why something worked and how it worked. My mother encouraged me to explore almost anything that interested me. She allowed me to take apart old clocks and radios so that I could figure out how they worked.

The more I learned, the more I wanted to know, which led me quickly to the discovery of the wealth of information available in books, plus the magical journeys I could take through the power of words!

Reading became the center of my life. The town library was located in the Women's Club of the little farming community that I called home. In my eyes, it was the grandest building in town - newly built, with a heavenly air-conditioner that sheltered me from the blazing heat of Arizona summers. It was my personal cocoon in which I could read the hours away.

My first adventure in writing came my senior year in high school when I decided to take a writing correspondence course, which was very forward-looking for the time. I experienced the first thrill of putting pen to paper. It was a magical new adventure! My love affair with the written word began.

Unfortunately, my affair was dealt a serious blow during my first year in college when an English professor told me that I used a lot of words, but said very little. His words went to my very core and hobbled my writing confidence for a number of years. I continued to write, but not with the same excitement and enthusiasm that I had previously enjoyed.

It was not until many years later that everything turned around. After completing my MBA as a "mature woman" I found a position with a Leadership Development Training Company in Manhattan that required use of three of my major passions: my insatiable curiosity of how and why things work, my love of learning through books, and my need to write and be published.

I know, my work was not published in the true sense of the word, but my words were in print and people were reading them and using them to improve their professional lives. I had finally begun to realize my dream.

Now I am retired and living the dream on a daily basis. I write many hours every day. All work is non-fiction. Even though I love fiction, that has never been my focus and there are others who do it so much better than I. My choice has always been, and will continue to be, to write about topics that interest and intrigue me and to share what I discover with my readers.

Other Books by this Author

Cookbooks

Candy Making Made Easy - Instructions and 17 Starter Recipes

Cake Making Made Easy - Instructions and 60 Cakes

Cook Ahead – Freezer to Table

The Healthy Diet Cookbook

Garden Fresh Soups and Stews

Mama's Legacy Series

Seven Volumes Available

Dinner – 55 Easy Recipes (Volume I)

Breakfast and Brunch – 60 Delicious Recipes (Volume II)

Dessert – 50 Scrumptious Choices (Volume III)

Chicken – 25 Classic Dinners (Volume IV)

Mexican Favorites – 21 Traditional Recipes (Volume V)

Side Dish Recipes (Volume VI)

Sauce Recipes – 50 Tasty Choices (Volume VII)

Health and Fitness

DETOX – The Master Cleanse Diet

The Secret to Successful Dieting

Juicing for Life

Business

Books Written Under Pen Names

www.ingramcontent.com/pod-product-compliance
Lightning Source LLC
Chambersburg PA
CBHW060412190526
45169CB00002B/860